AF444353

The kitten drinks from a cup.

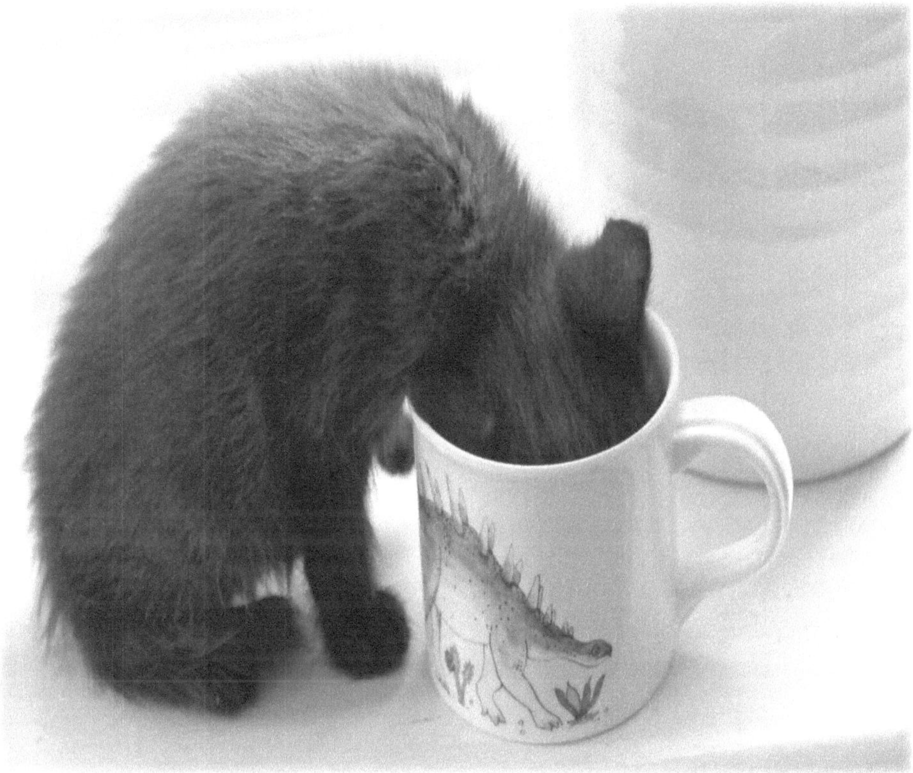

She is very little!

Kitten and her sister play.

They like to play in the sun.

Kitten and her sister eat.

They are hungry.

Now kitten and her sister want to sleep.

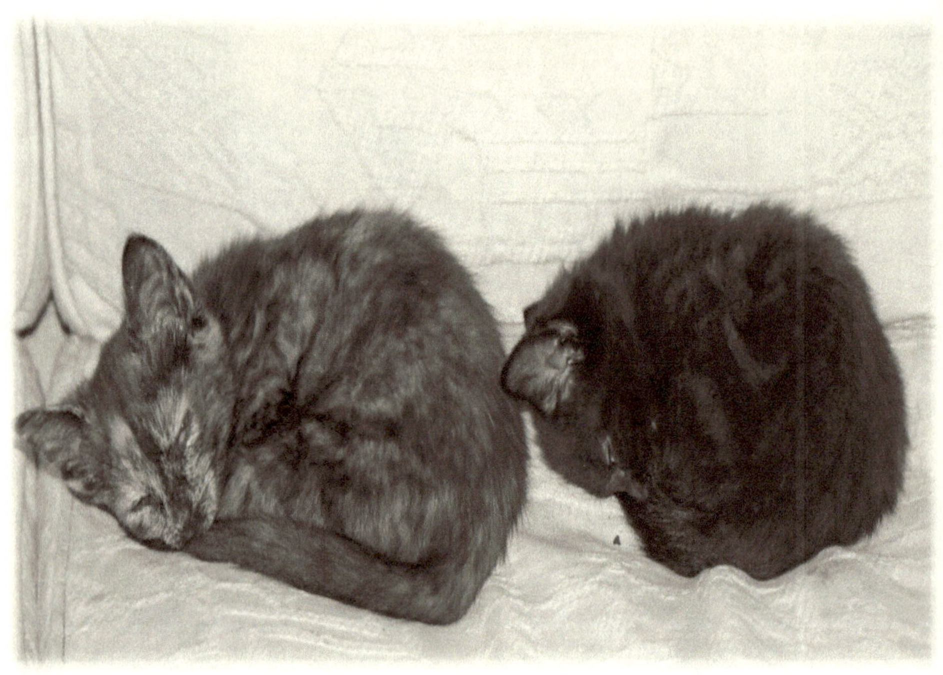

I like the kittens, don't you?

2. Pudgy Wants to Sleep

This is Pudgy. She has a good name.

She likes to sit on bags.

She is a funny cat!

She sees a bag. She has to sit on it.

Pudgy! You are so funny!

Pudgy wants to sleep.

Is this a good place? No, it's a bit hard.

Is this a good place?

No! It's a bit lumpy!

Pudgy can't find a good place.

Can her friends help her?

This is Patti. She is a black cat.

She likes to sit in the sun, but the chair
is hard.

Patti says the bricks are hard, too.

Patti, that's no good!

This is Tuffins.

Maybe he knows a good place?

Tuffins! Don't be silly! Rocks are no good!

Where can Pudgy sleep?

She likes a place that is warm and soft.

This is Chilli. Oh! She has found a good place to sleep. The bed is warm and soft.

Yes! Beds are very soft! Thank you, Chilli!

Now Pudgy can go to sleep. Good night!

3. Pudgy Looks for her Friends

Pudgy is bored. What can she do?

Where are her friends?
The sun is shining. Maybe they are
outside.

Patti is outside in the sun.

Tuffins is outside too. He is busy.

He is looking for a mouse!

Chilli wants to eat.

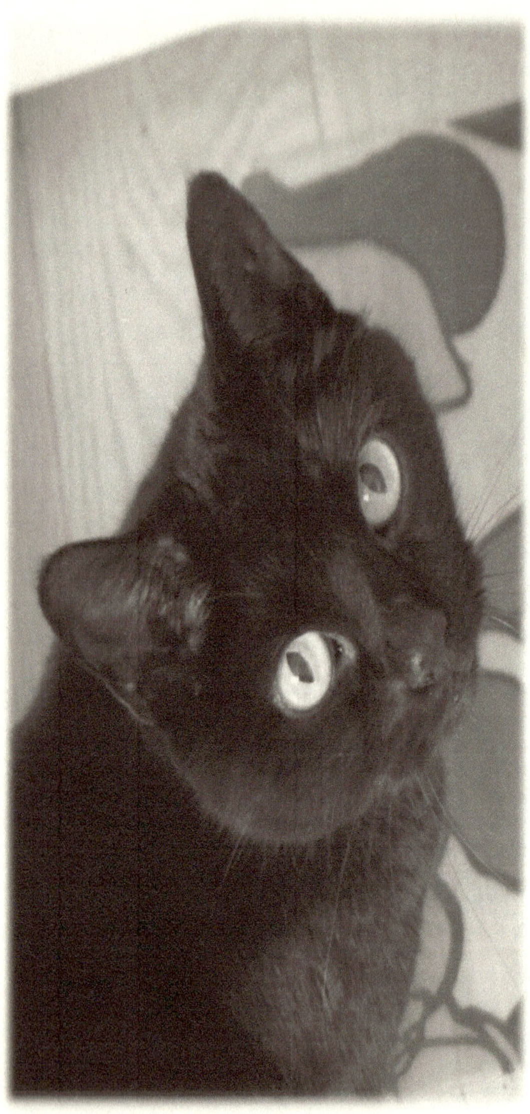

She says,

"Food, please!"

She doesn't want to go outside.

Pudgy looks for Patti.

Where is Patti? I don't see her.

Where can she be?

There she is! What is she doing?

Oh! She likes to eat catnip!
Look at her! She is so funny! Silly Patti!

Pudgy doesn't like catnip.

She likes to sit by the tree in the sun.

She dreams of
seeing her friend
Dibs, but he is
too far away.

He lives at the
beach now.
Lucky Dibs!

Words I have learned to read:

The cats in this book:

Pudgy   Patti

Tuffins   Chilli

Dibs

Words in this book:

"Kitten":

kitten (11)

the (8)

sister, is, a (4)

and, I, you, she, her, to, in, sleep, sun, like, on (3)

they, likes, don't, here, play, warm, little, are (2)

at, too, being, very, want, asleep, lap, lot, this, drinks,

eat, sits, cup, hungry, now, from, look, black, fast,

asleep (1)

"Pudgy wants to sleep":
(repeated from "Kitten")
a (12), she (11), is (10)
to, this (6)
the (4),
likes, sleep, are (3),
warm, and, on, very (2)
in, is, sun, you, now, chair, don't, her, too, black, so (1)

New words for "Pudgy wants to sleep":
good (9)
place (6)
no (4)
soft, has, sit, hard (3)
funny, that, bit, bed, sleep, can, warm, bag, wants (2)
yes, be, he, her, oh, cat, can't, where, go, but, it, help,
find, knows, says, sees, thank, silly, lumpy, night,
rocks, maybe, bricks, name, friends (1)

"Pudgy looks for her friends":
(Repeated from the first two stories)
s, she (10)
the, her (5)
to, he (4)
friend (3)
n, sun, likes, at, too, eat, can, look, are (2)
I, like, want, don't, now, he, oh, go, where, sit, wants,
silly, look, be, maybe, funny, silly, they (1)

New words for "Pudgy looks for her friends":
outside (4)
what, for, friends, looks (3)
catnip, doesn't (2)
bored, do, where, looking, shining, busy, mouse, says,
food, please, see, seeing, so, of, there, by, but, tree,
beach, doing, dreams, far, away, lives, lucky (1)

ABOUT THE AUTHOR

Annette Meredith is a master gardener, photographer and lifelong student of nature who is passionate about environmental issues and conservation. Born in the UK, she now lives in North Carolina, where she enjoys encouraging, observing and photographing nature as she works to improve sixty acres of woodland, meadows and organic gardens. She also enjoys writing stories that inspire children to love books and nature.

Other books by Annette Meredith:

"Nature on our Doorstep" series for children:

Saving the Bees	Helping the Hummingbirds
Birds in Our Back Yard	The Secret World of Flowers
Butterflies are Beautiful	Nature on Our Doorstep
Growing a Green Thumb	

More Books for Young Children:

Five First Rhyming Readers	Nature Rhymes

Other Books:

A Bluebird Story	A Nature Companion
Monarchs and Milkweed	All About My Cat

Books for the UK and Europe:

Birds in Our Back Garden	Nature on Our Doorstep	Growing Green Fingers

www.ingramcontent.com/pod-product-compliance
Lightning Source LLC
Chambersburg PA
CBHW020522160726
47991CB00007B/3078